Helen's Sweets and Treats

by

Helen Barrionuevo

ISBN-13: 978-1540590244
ISBN-10: 1540590240

Edited and formatted by bzhercules.com
Cover by LLPix Design

Disclaimer

In the writing of this cookbook, I have made every attempt to be true to my memories and to be totally honest in the province of the recipes. Most of my recipes have been passed down by family and friends and not in any formal way. I have boxes of recipes in my home, old and new. I have searched and weeded out my children's favorites and mine. I have made these the basis of this book. I apologize for any errors, omissions, etc.

Table of Contents

I am writing this cookbook so that my family and friends will have a solid written remembrance of me and how much I loved baking and how much I loved all of them. I know that some of them will recall the wonderful cookies that I loved to bake for them, especially my three sons.

My late husband used to say that my cookies tasted so good because they were "made with love" and I believe that he was right.

People have lost the art and fondness of made-from-scratch cookies, pies, cakes, and food in general. I think that it is a time thing. No one ever has enough time to deal with the forgotten niceties of life and they struggle to find time to complete the many day-to-day necessities in living their lives, myself included.

These are not low-fat, low-sugar recipes (except for one). These are old-fashioned standard ingredients—nothing instant (except for one pudding). They are not fancy or gourmet nor do they require an abundance of expensive ingredients to prepare. These are recipes that I have been baking for years.

There is such a deep satisfaction in my heart and soul when someone enjoys something that I have baked for them. I like to bake to say thank you, for an ill friend, for someone's party, for meetings, for all sorts of things. I especially love it when someone walks into my house and says, "Wow! That smells delicious!" It warms my heart.

When I told my daughter-in-law Kathie that I was writing this book, she said that she was going to make a cookbook for my grandson Michael of all of his favorites that she cooks for him. He just started college and is not liking his cafeteria's food too well. He may be cooking from his mom's cookbook soon! Good going, Michael; you can do it!

Helen Barrionuevo
December, 2015
Wellington, Florida

I am the mother of three wonderful grown men, Allan, Joe, and Brandon, the grandmother of two grandsons and a granddaughter, and hopefully, the adored mother-in-law of three loving daughters-in-law.

I have been cooking and baking ever since I can remember. As a teenager, I remember going to neighbors' houses to borrow ingredients to bake cookies with. I don't remember if those neighbors were ever reimbursed for their flour, sugar, butter, etc. While I enjoy cooking for friends and family, my passion in the kitchen is baking cookies. I think that maybe they are my favorites because they are just a little bite of something sweet. They are a lot easier to eat than, say, a slice of cake or pie. You can satisfy your sweet tooth without going crazy with the calories, if you can stop at one or two, that is, which oftentimes, I can't.

Baking cookies is a joy to me. There is nothing more fun on a cold and/or rainy/snowy day than to make cookies. There is joy in the mixing and baking and the lovely aroma that fills your home. It's like a prayer to me, as are art, music, reading, and sometimes meditating or visualizing. I think that God wanted us to enjoy life and do what pleases us and for us to nourish our loved ones in any way that we possibly can.

Years ago, when I lived in Chicago (which seems like another lifetime to me), I baked a lot more than I do now. The boys grew up in the suburbs of Chicago, where we had many long cold winters, rainy springs, beautiful falls, and of course, the long dark days of winter. The climate was a lot more conducive to baking than it is here in Florida where I live now. There were three hungry boys to clean the cookie jar in one sitting too.

In Chicago, I would start baking for Christmas as soon as Thanksgiving was over. Many times, I would come home from work, make dinner, and help the kids with homework, and then once the kids were asleep, I would bake. It soothed me, it gave me peace, it was a creative outlet, and everyone enjoyed the fruits of my labors. I would bake and freeze about twenty different batches of cookies. The kids sometimes ate them frozen, sneaking them out of the freezer. When Christmas came, I would make up trays of all of the beautiful cookies and give them to friends, take them to work, and even sell some for people having Christmas parties.

I have to give credit to my deceased girlfriend Lori for spurring me on in my baking endeavors. She had six kids and was a wonderful cook and baker, mother, wife, and friend. She started me on the cookie tray idea because she used to bake with her daughters and they would freeze and then make wonderful trays and share their bounty with friends and neighbors and I happened to be lucky enough to be a friend. She shared with me her expertise and many different cookie recipes.

The most important lesson that I learned from her was to read a recipe thoroughly before attempting to make it. The first step is to make sure that you have all of the necessary ingredients. I like to place all of the ingredients on the counter by my mixer to make sure that I have everything. Then I make sure to re-read it so that I follow the steps that are called for in the order that they are called for. It is also important to notice the degree of temperature for the oven. Most cookies call for pre-heated ovens. The timing of the baking is also important. Though all ovens bake differently, the times specified in a recipe depend on your oven, so the timing is just a general guide. You will have to check the cookies occasionally for the exact timing.

Have fun baking!
Enjoy yourself,

Helen Barrionuevo

Alyce's Chocolate Chip Cookies

My sister Alyce is a wonderful gourmet cook and baker. She does a zillion things in a day. She is a person of many talents: choir director, piano player, and teacher of piano playing. She cooks for the homeless, is very involved in her church, author of her first cookbook, *Soup and Sides*, which is an excellent cookbook with wine pairings and desserts as well as delicious hearty soups. Alyce is a fantastic wife, mother, grandmother, and sister. She is well traveled and very well educated. These cookies are just one of the many delicious things that she makes. This recipe is for my favorite cookie of all time.

Helen Barrionuevo

1 ¼ cup butter

1 ½ cup flour

¾ cup brown sugar

1 tsp. baking soda

½ cup sugar

1 tsp. salt

1 egg

3 cups uncooked oatmeal, whirl in blender until pulverized

1 tsp. vanilla

6 oz. chocolate chips

¾ cups chopped nuts

Preheat oven to 375°

In a large mixing bowl, beat together butter and sugars until light and fluffy. Beat in egg and vanilla. In separate bowl, combine flour, baking soda, and salt and oatmeal. Mix the flour mixture into the butter mixture. Add chocolate chips and chopped nuts. Mix all together.

Drop by rounded tsp. on ungreased cookie sheet.

Bake at 375 for 8-10 minutes.

Let cool in the pan for 1 minute, then transfer to racks to cool completely.

Makes 6 dozen

Apricot Nut Cups

This is a recipe shared with me by one of my dear friends, Vivian Lovcik. She is an excellent cook and an even better baker. She just seems to have that extra touch when it comes to entertaining and making delicious food and desserts.

She is a great friend and has been through hell and back with me when I needed someone so badly by my side several years ago. I owe her a great deal of gratitude and I truly value her friendship as a gift from God.

Pastry:
3 oz. cream cheese (softened)
½ cup butter
1 cup flour

Preheat oven to 350°.

Blend softened cream cheese and butter into flour with a pastry blender. Form 24 1-inch balls with floured hands. Line miniature muffin pans with balls of dough and shape into cups.

Filling:
1 egg
½ cup brown sugar
½ jar Baker's apricot filling
½ cup chopped nuts

Combine all the ingredients. Spoon into muffin cups and bake for 20 minutes. Let cool in the pan and gently remove with a tsp.

Makes 24 cups.

Butter Cookie Cut Outs

Years ago, one of my friend's daughters made these cookies and shared the recipe with me. It is one of the best plain butter cookies that I have ever tasted. Crisp yet creamy and just the right amount of buttery heaven.

1 cup butter (softened)
1 cup sugar
1 egg
2 tbsp. orange juice
1 tsp. vanilla
2 ½ cups flour
1 tsp. baking powder

Frosting:
3 cups powdered sugar
⅓ cup butter (softened)
1 tsp. vanilla
1 to 2 tbsp. milk

Cream butter, sugar, and egg in a large mixer bowl. Beat at medium speed, scraping the bowl often. Add orange juice and vanilla and blend well. Add flour and baking powder; reduce speed to low and mix well.
Divide dough into thirds and wrap in saran wrap and refrigerate for 2-3 hours.

Preheat oven to 400°

Take one package of dough out of the refrigerator at one time. Roll the dough out on a well-floured surface to about ¼-inch thickness. Cut the dough with cookie cutters of your choice dipped in flour. Carefully remove cookies with a spatula onto parchment-lined cookie sheets. Bake 6-10 minutes or until cookies are slightly browned. Let cookies sit on the pan for 2 minutes and then carefully transfer them by spatula to wire cookie racks to cool completely.

For Frosting:
Beat powdered sugar, ⅓ cup butter, and 1 tsp. of vanilla in small bowl. Beat at low speed, scraping sides of bowl often. Add enough milk to make it spreading consistency.
Frost and decorate cookies as you prefer.

Makes 3 dozen cookies

Candied Christmas Pecans

These are a tasty, crispy addition to a tray of cookies or just as a treat served in small pretty bowls around the party for a sweet treat. The recipe was originally created by Carolyne Roehm.

1 lb. pecan halves
1 egg white
1 tsp. cold water
1 cup sugar
1 tsp. cinnamon
1 tsp. salt

Preheat the oven to 250°.

Beat egg white with water until fluffy. Fold pecans into egg whites until well coated.

Mix cinnamon, sugar, and salt in large bowl. Fold the coated pecans into the sugar/cinnamon mixture. Bake on a parchment-lined cookie sheet for one hour. Your home will smell wonderful. Cool thoroughly and break any big pieces apart. Store in an airtight container.

Cherry Almond Balls

This recipe has been around a long time. I lost the original one that I had and it was a very easy one to follow and bake. I recently ran across this very similar one in our 2010 Commemorative Cookbook for my church, St. Therese de Lisieux in Wellington, Florida. It was entered by Frances Wallin. The cookies are small, tender, and delicious.

¾ cup butter
⅓ cup confectioner sugar
1 tsp. vanilla
¼ tsp. salt
2 cups sifted all-purpose flour
½ cup almonds, finely chopped
Whole candied cherries, approx. 60

Preheat oven to 325°.

Cream together, butter, confectioner's sugar, vanilla, and salt until light and fluffy. Add flour and almonds. Mix well. Use a teaspoonful of dough to roll around each candied cherry. Place on a parchment-lined cookie sheet. Bake for 30 minutes. Cool slightly and roll in additional sifted confectioner sugar.

Makes about 5 dozen cookies.

Chocolate Chip Cups

This recipe was graciously shared with me by an old and dear friend, Marge Dankert. She was a cake maker and decorator extraordinaire. She made and decorated beautiful and delicious cakes in her tiny little kitchen in Carpentersville, IL and later in Aurora, Co. I could never understand how she could so quickly bake and beautifully decorate a five- or six-layer cake at seemingly a moment's notice. We shared many hours of fun and laughter together while she was teaching me the basics of cake decorating (which I still don't do well today) and also teaching me how to crochet, which I have no patience for at all. We also spent lots of time eating and playing Rummy K with our families. Her two girls were the same ages as my two boys and we had great times together.

1 8-ounce package of cream cheese (softened)
1 egg
1 ⅓ cup sugar
1 6-ounce package of semi-sweet chocolate chips
1 tsp. vanilla
1 ½ cups sifted flour
¼ cup unsweetened cocoa
1 tsp. baking soda
⅓ cup cooking oil
1 cup water
1 tbsp. vinegar
⅛ tsp. salt and ½ tsp. salt

Preheat oven to 350°

Sift together flour, 1 cup sugar, cocoa, baking soda, and ½ tsp. salt. Add water, oil, vinegar, and vanilla. Beat until well blended.

Line, or grease and flour two mini-muffin tins, set aside.

Combine cream cheese, egg, ⅓ cup of sugar and ⅛ tsp. salt and beat well with electric mixer. Stir in chocolate chips and set aside.

Fill muffin tins ⅓ full with the cocoa mixture. Place a heaping tsp. of the cream cheese mixture on top of the cocoa mixture.

Bake at 350° for 12-15 minutes.

Recipe makes 36 individual cups.

Chocolate Kiss Macaroons

Many years ago, I came upon this recipe somewhere and wrote it down, as I often do with something that sounds good and I think that I might try some day. I have often made these over the years for special events and have always gotten raves. This is one of the cookies that always went on my cookie trays in Chicago and disappeared first.

⅔ cups butter
6 oz. creamed cheese (softened)
1 ½ cups sugar
2 egg yolks
1 tsp. vanilla
1tbsp. orange juice
2 ½ cups flour
1 tbsp. + 1 tsp. of baking powder
½ tsp. salt
10 cups of flaked coconut in 6-cup and 4-cup increments
1 bag Hershey Kisses

Cream butter, cream cheese, and sugar until light and fluffy. Beat in vanilla, egg yolks, and orange juice until creamy.

In a medium bowl, mix flour, salt, baking powder.

Beat in flour mixture gradually into butter mixture. Beat in the 6 cups of coconut into the cream/flour mixture.

Refrigerate dough for 1 hour and, in the meantime, unwrap Hershey kisses.

Preheat oven to 350°.

Roll 1 ½-inch balls out of dough. Roll these balls in the 4 cups of coconut, pressing into the dough. Place on parchment-lined cookie sheets and bake for 12-14 minutes until the cookies puff up and are very slightly browned.

Remove from oven and press a Hershey's Kiss on each cookie. Return pan to oven and bake another 2 minutes.

Remove cookies carefully with a spatula onto a cooling rack and cool completely.

Will keep well for a week in an airtight container.

Chocolate Snowballs

This is a Betty Crocker cookie recipe that I just love to make and it is an easy, fun cookie to add to a holiday cookie tray and I always get rave reviews when I serve it!

> 1 pouch (1 lb. 1.5 ounce) Betty Crocker Sugar Cookie Mix
> ½ cup butter or margarine melted
> 1 egg
> ¼ cup all-purpose flour
> ¼ cup unsweetened cocoa powder
> ½ cup finely chopped almonds
> 1 tsp. almond extract
> 60 Hershey's Kisses unwrapped
> ¾ cup powdered sugar

Preheat oven to 375°.

In a large bowl, stir cookie mix, butter, egg, flour, cocoa, almonds, and extract until a soft dough firms.

Shape dough into 60 ¾-inch balls. Wrap each ball around a Hershey's Kiss. Place 2 inches apart on an ungreased cookie sheet.

Bake 8 to 10 minutes or until set. Immediately remove from cookie sheet. Cool slightly, about 5 minutes.

Roll cookies in powdered sugar. Cool completely, about 15 minutes. Reroll cookies in powdered sugar. Store tightly covered.

Makes 60 cookies and will take about 20 minutes to make.

Crispy, Crunchy, Peanut Butter Cookies

I have never been a fan of peanut butter, I just don't like it and never did. These were my kids' favorite cookies while they were growing up. I haven't made them in a long time. A few weeks ago, my son and daughter-in-law went to parents' weekend at my grandson's college and I sent a batch to him, remembering how much he likes them. My daughter-in-law, who is not a sweets eater, even ate a few and declared them exceptional. It makes my heart sing when my kids and grandkids enjoy something that I make, especially when I know it is their favorite. It is a wonderful way to show that you love them.

½ cup butter, room temperature
1 tbsp. milk
1 cup crunchy peanut butter
1 tsp. vanilla
¾ cup sugar, more for rolling them
1¼ cup flour
½ cup brown sugar
1 tsp. baking soda
1 egg
½ tsp. baking powder
½ cup finely chopped salted peanuts
¼ tsp. salt

Preheat oven to 350°

Line two baking sheets with parchment paper.

Cream butter, peanut butter, and brown sugar together until light and fluffy. Add egg, vanilla, and milk and beat some more.

In a separate bowl, blend the flour, baking powder, baking soda, and salt until well mixed.

Place the flour mixture in the butter mixture and beat until well mixed. Fold in the chopped peanuts.

Roll one-tbsp.-size balls in your hands and then dip in a small bowl of the extra sugar to coat well. Place the balls on the baking sheet and with a fork dipped in sugar make a cross of the times pressing down to flatten the cookie slightly.

Bake at 350° for 8-10 minutes. Do not let them get too brown. Let sit for a minute on the pans and then remove them to cooling racks to cool.

Makes 3 dozen cookies

Dreamsicle Cake

I have had this recipe in my recipe box for years. Every once in a while, I will think about it and make it. It is a great cake to take to church suppers for dessert. It is moist and dense and everyone just loves it. It reminds me of the Dreamsicles that I used to have as a kid, or maybe they were called Creamsicles; whatever, this cake is delicious and easy. It is a little time consuming because you have to let both the cake and the frosting chill, but it is worth the effort.

The Cake:
1 (18 oz.) box of orange cake mix
1 (3 oz. box of orange Jell-O)
⅓ cup vegetable oil
3 eggs
1 tsp. orange extract
1¼ cups water

The Icing
8 ounces sour cream
½ cup shredded coconut
1¼ cups sugar
½ cup orange juice
8 ounces Cool Whip (or Whipped Cream, if you prefer)

Preheat oven to 350°

The Cake

Combine cake mix, Jell-O, vegetable oil, eggs, orange extract, and water in a large bowl. Beat with an electric mixer until fully blended, about 2 minutes.

Flour and grease two 9-inch cake pans. Pour cake mixture into pans and bake in a preheated 350° oven for 25 minutes or until a toothpick inserted into cake comes out clean.

Cool in pans completely on a wired rack. Remove from pans and wrap tightly in plastic wrap. Place in the refrigerator for several hours to firm up.

The Icing

Combine sour cream and coconut and a small bowl. In another small bowl, combine orange juice and sugar until sugar is dissolved. Add the orange juice mixture to the sour cream, stirring until blended. Fold into Cool Whip or your own whipped cream. Cover and chill for several hours.

Unwrap the cake and slice each into two layers; you will have four layers of cake. Place on a plate and spread icing on first layer, repeat with three more layers. Frost sides and top to complete frosting the cake!

Delicious!

Greek Rice Pudding

In my past life, I was a waitress in the Northwest suburbs of Chicago and, for most of those years, I worked in Greek fine dining restaurants. Greek people, for the most part, are wonderful family people and great cooks. They can be hot tempered and fiery sometimes, but on the inside, they are pushovers.

In the last restaurant I worked, the Greek chef made wonderful rice pudding. I would come in from the cold on a blistery Chicago morning and he would have made a huge pot of rice pudding. I could smell it when I first walked in the door. The thought of it was warming in itself. He would always put a little bowl aside for me and sprinkle cinnamon on it. It warmed me inside and out. Most people like it cold, but I like it warm, kind of like oatmeal.

Now, although I live in Florida and our winters are always very mild, I do make the rice pudding and eat it cold. There is nothing as cold as a Chicago morning with the wind whipping off of the lake. This pudding really took the chill off rapidly.

After much coercing, one of my bosses' wives gave me her recipe, family size so that I could make it for my family. Her name was Sophia and I share her recipe here with you today.

½ gallon milk
1 cup sugar
1 cup uncooked long grain white rice
3 eggs, slightly beaten
¼ cup milk
¼ tsp. salt
2 tsp. vanilla extract

Helen Barrionuevo
Ground cinnamon to taste

In a large pan over medium-low heat, combine rice, milk, and sugar. Bring to a simmer and simmer one hour covered. Stir often so it doesn't stick to bottom of pan. Remove from heat.

In a small bowl, combine ¼ cup milk, eggs, salt, and vanilla. Stir into the rice mixture and cook for 2 minutes, stirring constantly.

Pour into a 9X13 inch dish or pan and cover with plastic wrap. Let steam out by folding back corners of plastic wrap. Let cool at room temperature. When the pudding has cooled, remove plastic wrap and sprinkle with cinnamon. Recover with new plastic wrap and refrigerate until cold. Serve in individual dishes. To add a little pizzazz, place whipped cream on top and sprinkle with more cinnamon.

It will make about 8 good-sized servings.

All totaled, it will take about 75 minutes to make until finished.

Flo's Mexican Brownies

This recipe was shared with me from a very special lady who departed this earth way too early. I only knew her for a short time, less than a year, but she made a lasting impression on me.

She always had a smile for everyone. She loved to cook and she loved to eat at home or out on the town. She was new to our neighborhood and my friend Sue and I took her to our Red Hat outings and she loved them. She was a people person and in the short time that she was here in our neighborhood, she found joy and friendship.

These brownies are moist and have a little extra spice to them that you don't normally find in typical brownies. It adds another layer of goodness to an original favorite. They don't need frosting; they are rich and delicious by themselves.

½ lb. butter
2 cups sugar
4 large eggs
2 tsp. vanilla extract
⅔ cup unsweetened cocoa powder
1 cup flour
1 tsp. ground cinnamon
¼ tsp. chili powder
½ tsp. salt
½ tsp. baking powder

Preheat oven to 350°.

Line a 9/13 pan with parchment paper, leaving an overhang on the two long sides. Press the parchment paper into the corners of the pan and lightly grease the pan with a slight amount of butter.

Melt the butter in a large saucepan over medium-low heat. Remove the pan from heat and cool slightly. Add the sugar, eggs, and vanilla to the saucepan and stir with a wooden spoon until combined.

Add the cocoa, flour, cinnamon, chili powder, salt, and baking powder into ingredients in the saucepan and mix until smooth.

Spread the batter in the prepared pan and lightly move the pan until all areas of the bottom are covered.

Bake 20-25 minutes until a toothpick inserted into the brownies comes out fudgy. Cool in the pan on a rack. Once cool, use the parchment paper to lift out the brownies. If you like, you could sprinkle the brownies with powdered sugar, but it is not necessary.

Cut into 18 pieces and enjoy!

Fools Toffee

This recipe is a surprise. When I first read this recipe I thought, *no way, this can't be anything similar to toffee*, but I was really surprised once I tried out the recipe. It is sweet, easy to prepare, and tastes just like toffee that would normally take a few hours to make! I had clipped this recipe out of a newspaper years ago and didn't get around to trying it until a few years ago and it was truly a surprise.

2 cups butter
1 cup packed dark brown sugar
36 2x2 inch saltine crackers
11½ ounces chocolate chips
½ cup chopped pecans

Preheat oven to 375°.

In a small saucepan over medium heat, blend butter and brown sugar. Heat to boiling and boil for 4 minutes. Cover a 10" by 15" jellyroll pan with aluminum foil and butter the foil lightly. Place single layer of saltines side by side on foil close together. Pour butter mixture over saltine crackers, spread evenly.

Bake in a 375° oven for 5 minutes. Immediately remove from oven and sprinkle chocolate chips over saltines. Allow chips to melt and gently spread over saltines. Sprinkle with chocolate chips. Refrigerate until cool. Break into uneven pieces once cooled. May be kept in covered container for a week or so in refrigerator.

Makes 3-4 dozen cookies.

Ice Box Cookies from Kauai

Recently, I had the opportunity to visit Kauai, one of the Hawaiian Islands. I had been there several years ago and had always wanted to go back. Kauai called to my heart and soul when I was there. The first visit was with my two sisters and we had taken a tour of all of the Hawaiian Islands by cruise ship. We had only spent one day in Kauai and part of that day was spent in a helicopter viewing the mountains, waterfalls, and the Napali Coast from above. This time, I got to see all of Kauai in its natural beauty from eye level and it is truly a beautiful island. It is so lush and green with beautiful trees and flowers, ocean and mountains and all of God's creations right at my fingertips. I feel that Kauai is a very spiritual place, for me anyway. It is ancient and I feel that I am closer to God there with the gentle breezes blowing and the beautiful coastline and mountains.

One afternoon, we visited an old sugar plantation on the island; in fact, one of the first sugar plantations to be built there. It is called Grove Farm and it had been renovated into a museum in the last several years. It was built in 1864 and started as a small building with a thatched roof and was added on to over the years until it became the huge plantation that it was. It was owned by George Wilcox and his three daughters. It was restored with a lot of the original furniture and knick-knacks and even old books and financial ledgers.

The afternoon that we were there, we were treated to an old cookie that the daughters of George Wilcox used to make on their wood burning stove. One of the docents made these lovely cookies for us. They were crispy, crunchy, and small, almost delicate. They were a perfect afternoon treat with a glass of minted iced tea. She even shared the recipe with us. The recipe is as follows…

½ cup butter
2¾ cup all-purpose flour
1½ cup raw sugar
1 tsp. baking soda
2 beaten eggs
1 tsp. vanilla

Mix all ingredients together with an electric mixer. When mixed roll into a log about the size of a quarter and place the roll on waxed paper and roll up the waxed paper. Place into refrigerator about 2 hours to chill.

Pre-heat oven to 325°

When ready to bake; grease cookie sheet and cut thin slices, about ½ inch wide, off of the log. Place about one inch apart on cookie sheet for baking.

Bake 20-25 minutes at 325°. Cookies will appear very lightly browned when done. Remove from cookie sheet immediately wire racks. It will make about 2½ dozen cookies.

Lemon Dreams

This recipe was shared with me by a dear friend and a superb Polish cook and baker, Lori Gundlach, and was passed down from her grandmother to her. The whole family loved to bake and entertain. She had six children and there was always something in the oven, on the stove, or being served at their house. The house was run very well; each child had their own chores and they were all wonderful kids. The girls grew up passing down the families' recipes to their children as well.

These lemon cookies are light and tender, similar to a shortbread cookie. They melt in your mouth. They go great with a cup of coffee or tea or just by themselves.

Cookies:
1¼ cups all-purpose flour
¾ cups of softened butter
½ cup cornstarch
⅓ cup powdered sugar
1 tbsp. lemon juice
1 tsp. freshly grated lemon juice

Frosting:
¾ cup powdered sugar
¼ cup softened butter
1 tsp. freshly grated lemon peel
1 tsp. lemon juice

Combine all cookie ingredients in large mixing bowl. Beat at low speed until well combined making sure to scrape sides of bowl.

Divide bowl in half. Shape each half into 8x1 inch logs. Wrap each log with plastic wrap and refrigerate for a few hours until firm.

Preheat oven to 350°.

Cut each log into ¼-inch slices with sharp knife. Place 2 inches apart on parchment lined cookie sheet. Bake 10 to 12 minutes or until firm. Cookies will not burn. Cool completely.

Combine all frosting ingredients in small bowl. Beat at medium speed until fluffy. .Frost cooled cookies.

Recipe makes 4 dozen cookies

Pastelitos De Boda (Mexican Wedding Cakes)

These little tidbits go by many different names. Pecan Balls, Pecan Crescents, Pecan Sticks, but I always refer to them as *Pastelitos De Boda* because the name has meaning for me. I found this recipe in a book that was simply named *Cook Book, Favorite Recipes from Our Best Cooks*. The author of the recipe is Hilda Garrido.

Several years ago, my stepson got married in Mexico City and, naturally, we attended the wedding. It was a lovely affair in a beautiful setting and was well catered. My husband and I wanted to contribute the appetizers and things for the sweet table for the wedding. We wanted some of the food to be American, made by us. We decided on mini barbequed ribs for the appetizers and several cookies and candies for the sweet table.

I found this recipe in an old cookbook that someone had given me and was very proud that I could make this Mexican cookie for the wedding reception. To my astonishment, no one in Mexico had ever tasted them or heard of them, but they all loved them. They were so impressed that we had made all of these things at home and drove with them intact to Mexico City.

¾ cup butter
4 tbsp. of powdered sugar
2 tsp. of vanilla
1 tsp. of cold water
2 cups of flour
⅛ tsp. salt

Helen Barrionuevo

1 cup finely chopped pecans
2 cups powdered sugar

Cream butter until fluffy; add sugar, vanilla, and cold water. Mix well and then add flour, salt and nuts. Shape into a roll about 1½ inches in diameter. Wrap in plastic wrap and chill for three hours. Cut into ¼-inch slices and place on parchment lined cookie sheet.

Preheat oven to 400°

Bake at 400° for 6-8 minutes or until lightly browned. Remove from baking sheet and roll in powdered sugar while still hot. Place on rack to cool. Roll again in powdered sugar once well cooled.

Makes 3 ½ to 4 dozen.

Pecan Tassies

I love these little individual cookies. They remind me of tiny pecan pies. Melt in your mouth goodness and bite size so you can indulge just a little because they are small, like a perfect mouthful.

I don't remember where this recipe came from. I have had it written by my own hand for many years now. It is simple to make and looks very elegant on a cookie tray.

> 1 cup butter (softened)
> 2 cups flour
> 1 8-ounce pkg. cream cheese (softened)

Beat flour, butter, and cream cheese together until combined. Chill for 2 hours.

Preheat oven to 350°

> 2 eggs
> 2 cups brown sugar
> 2 cups chopped pecans
> 2 tbsp. melted butter

Beat eggs, sugar, pecans and butter well.

Roll pastry into 1-inch balls. Place balls into small muffin tins and press pastry down slightly with thumb. Fill dough with 1 teaspoonful of pecan mixture.

Bake at 350° in a pre-heated oven for 20 minutes.

Let cool on wire racks and then remove from pans.

Makes 3 dozen or more tarts.

Potato Chip Cookies

This cookie is my favorite one of all time. Years ago in Chicago, my friend Lori and her three daughters used to start making Christmas cookies around Halloween and then freeze them. When Christmas came, all of their friends and families would get a huge tray of cookies. There would be twenty or so different kinds on each tray. It was always a nice treat to look forward to right before Christmas and to have all of the cookies available for whoever dropped in to have a few. This is a plain, easy cookie to make, but so delicious.

Preheat oven to 350°

> 1 cup butter, room temperature
> 1 cup margarine, room temperature
> 1 cup sugar
> 2 tsp. vanilla
> 3½ cups flour
> 1½ crushed potato chips
> 1 cup finely chopped pecans
> 2 cups powdered sugar

Cream butter and margarine (softened) well, beat in sugar, and add 2 tsp. vanilla. In a large bowl mix flour and crushed potato chips well. Gradually add the flour mixture into the butter/margarine mixture just until all is moistened. Fold in chopped pecans mixing well. Drop by teaspoonfuls onto a cookie sheet lined with parchment paper. They should look like little ragged mountains.

Bake at 350° for 15-20 minutes or until very lightly browned. Let sit 1 minute on cookie sheet and then transfer to wire racks to cool. When thoroughly cool sift powdered sugar over cookies.

Will be best stored in an airtight container for up to two weeks. These cookies can be easily frozen as well in the same container.

Will make ¾ dozen.
Enjoy!

Praline Cookie Bars

This cookie recipe has been around for some time. I hadn't made it in quite some time and had forgotten just how delicious that it was. I don't remember where the original recipe came from, but I found it again recently. I took it for our annual cookie exchange. It was a great hit and it makes a lot of cookie bars in a short time and is fairly easy, even for a beginner. It really has the rich, nutty flavor of pralines, which I have loved since my childhood.

Cookie Base:
1 cup unsalted butter
⅔ cup light brown sugar
2⅔ cup all-purpose flour
½ tsp. salt
½ cup finely ground pecans

Topping:
½ cup unsalted butter
1 cup light brown sugar
⅓ cup honey
2 tbsp. heavy cream
2 cups chopped pecans

Preheat oven to 350°.

Line a 9x13 baking pan with foil, making sure that the foil is larger than the pan and hangs over the sides.

Cookie Base

Cream the 1 cup of butter and brown sugar together. Slowly stir in the flower, salt, and ground pecans until the mixture is crumbly. Press into foil-lined pan and smooth it out with hands. Bake for 20 minutes until light golden brown.

Topping

Prepare topping while crust is baking.

Combine ½ cup butter, 1 cup of brown sugar, honey and heavy cream in a saucepan. Dissolve ingredients on. Lower heat and simmer for 1 minute on medium heat stirring constantly.

Pour topping over crust as soon as you remove it from the oven. Spread it out evenly

Return pan to the oven and bake for 20 minutes until the topping is set.

Remove pan from oven and let cool.

Use tin foil to lift the cookies out of the pan and. Remove the foil and cut cookies into 2"x 2" bars.

Enjoy!

Pumpkin Roll Cake

This recipe is a very special recipe. It was shared with me via my sister's mother-in-law, Lorna Morgan. I have made it every Thanksgiving since she first shared it with me. It is a little time consuming but worth all of the steps to make a great pumpkin dessert, especially if you are tired of or don't care for the traditional pumpkin pie! It looks beautiful and elegant on a serving plate!

Cake:
3 eggs
1 cup sugar
⅔ cup pumpkin
1 tsp. lemon juice
¾ cups flour
1 tsp. baking powder
2 tsp. cinnamon
1 tsp. ginger
½ tsp. nutmeg
1½ tsp. salt
1 cup finely chopped nuts

Preheat oven to 375°.

Beat 3 eggs on high for 5 minutes. Add sugar gradually. Stir in ⅔ cup pumpkin and add 1 tsp. of lemon juice and set aside. Stir together all dry ingredients and fold into pumpkin mixture. Grease a jellyroll pan and line with a piece of waxed paper the size of the pan. Pour the pumpkin mixture onto the waxed paper, leveling it out with a spatula. Gently hit the pan on top of the counter to get out air bubbles. Place chopped nuts on top of pumpkin mixture.

Bake at 375 for 15 minutes. Let cool for 5 minutes. Sprinkle a dishtowel with powdered sugar and turn the cake onto the dishtowel. Remove the waxed paper carefully. Turn the cake over onto the dishtowel and sprinkle with more powdered sugar. Roll up the dishtowel starting at the narrow end and let the cake cool this way for at least a couple of hours and unroll.

Filling:
6 ounces cream cheese (softened)
4 tbsp. margarine
½ tsp. vanilla
1 cup powdered sugar

Beat the first three ingredients until smooth. Slowly incorporate powdered sugar until smooth. Spread filling over unrolled cake and roll it up again. Keep chilled until ready to use. Slice into ¾-inch slices before serving and dust with powdered sugar.

Makes about 10 slices.

Rose's Biscotti

I have made these cookies many times over the years and this is my very favorite biscotti recipe to make.

I belong to a spiritual group called the Companions. I have baked these and shared them with the group a few times. My very dear friend and mentor, Luciana, happened to take a few to her mother Rose one evening. Her mother Rose was one hundred years old at the time and she really enjoyed them. She said that they reminded her of the biscotti that she used to bake for her own Italian family. That was a very high compliment to me. I made them a few more times for her before she went to meet her maker and she would share them with her friends in the assisted-living facility. Whenever I make them, I think of Rose and how much she enjoyed them, so I have named them after her!

> 3½ cups all-purpose flour
> 1 tsp. baking powder
> ½ tsp. salt
> ½ cup unsalted butter (at room temperature)

¾ cup sugar
3 eggs
1 tsp. vanilla extract
¾ cup dried cranberries

Preheat oven to 350°

In a small bowl, sift together flour, baking powder, and salt. Set aside

Combine butter, and sugar in a large mixing bowl. Beat until light and fluffy about 4 minutes. Add eggs one at a time, making sure to beat well after each addition of egg. Add the vanilla and beat. Incorporate the flour mixture into the wet ingredients and beat well. Add the dried cranberries and mix thoroughly.

Cut dough in half and shape into two large logs. They should be about 12 inches long and 1 inch thick.

Place on parchment-lined cookie sheet and bake about 30-35 minutes until just starting to brown around the edges. Let cool a few minutes on the baking sheet. While still warm, slice on the diagonal into ½-inch slices. Place cookies back on the baking sheet, and bake 7 to 10 minutes. Remove the pan and turn the cookies over and bake on the other side for 7 to 10 minutes. They should be fairly dry and crisp.

Let cookies cool on sheets and store in an airtight container for up to two weeks.

Makes 50 biscotti.
The biscotti will take about an hour to make.

Snickerdoodle

When I was a young girl, around seven or eight, I used to help one of our neighbors dust and vacuum her home on Saturdays. It was a job I loved. Her name was Myrtle and she was kind of an eccentric older lady to say the least. I enjoyed going to her home and she always fed me well. She had a huge walk-in closet, which was a very unusual thing in those days. In this closet, besides the usual things you keep in a closet, she kept homemade cookies, fudge, and candy. She called this closet "The Stash Box" and the treats that she kept in there were her husband Art's "noshes."

They had a tiny, lovely, cozy home that I admired. This home had a tiny kitchen too. It amazed me then and still amazes me now how she managed to bake such wonderful cookies and fudge in that kitchen. She was a baker but not a cook. She hated to cook and rarely did except for the occasional meatloaf or pot of spaghetti.

My salary for working on Saturday afternoons was to be able to pick any cookie or sweet thing that I wanted out of her husband's stash plus a dime. My favorite was the Snickerdoodle cookies that she made. I didn't really care about the dime much.

I have long since lost the recipe for the cookies and have tried several times to replicate the exact flavor and texture of them. I came upon this recipe in a 1902 community cookbook from Estherville, Iowa.

2⅔ cups all-purpose flour
2 tsp. cream of tartar
1 tsp. baking soda
½ tsp. salt

½ tsp. ground nutmeg
1 cup unsalted butter (slightly softened)
1¾ cups sugar
1½ tsp. light corn syrup
2 large eggs
2 tsp. vanilla extract
¼ cup sugar and 1½ tsp. cinnamon combined for topping.

Preheat oven to 375°.

Line several baking sheets with parchment paper.

In a large bowl, mix flour, cream of tartar, baking soda, salt, and nutmeg. In another large bowl, beat together butter, eggs, corn syrup, and vanilla on medium speed until creamy. Beat in half of the flour mixture until thoroughly moistened. Beat in the rest of the flour mixture. Cover the bowl with saran wrap and let sit in the refrigerator for 1 hour.

Roll the dough into 1½-inch balls with slightly greased hands. Roll the balls into the cinnamon/sugar mixture. Place about 2⅔ inches apart on the baking sheets. Slightly press down on cookies with your hand.

Bake the cookies, one sheet at a time, in the upper third of the oven for 8 to 10 minutes. Reverse the sheet from back to front about halfway through to insure even baking. Bake until the cookies are light golden brown around the edges. Place the cookie sheet on a wire rack to cool for a few minutes and then lift cookies with a spatula onto another wire rack to cool completely.

May be stored in an airtight container for ten days or frozen for two months.

Sue's Banana Pudding

My dear friend Sue is an incredible baker. She enjoys trying new recipes and sharing the bounty with her friends. She also puts them in pretty boxes or decorative plates or cookie bags, just to make them a special gift. It is like getting two beautiful gifts in one. She shares a lot of her baking bounty with our friends and relatives. It is always a delight to receive something that Sue has baked, and it is always something delicious.

This is a quick, easy, low cal, low fat recipe and it tastes like the banana pudding that my mom used to make.

> 1 5.5-oz. sugar-free vanilla instant pudding
> (Jell-O or Royal brand)
> 3 cups cold skim milk
> 1 8-oz. sugar-free Cool Whip
> 4 ripe bananas, sliced

Prepare pudding according to package directions using the 3 cups of cold skim milk, beating with a whisk (not an electric mixer) approximately 2 minutes. Fold in half of the sugar-free Cool Whip and all of the sliced bananas. Pour into serving dishes, cover, and refrigerate. When ready to serve, garnish with the remaining sugar-free Cool Whip.

Tuscany Biscotti

(In Italian, it is "*cantuccini*")

I like biscotti. It is flavorful, a little dry, and begs to be dipped in Italian sweet wine, coffee, or a nice cold glass of milk. There are many different flavors of biscotti and I have tried several and I enjoy baking them so much. It gives me joy to bake these and to eat them as well.

2 cups flour
¾ cup sugar
1 ½ tsp baking powder
½ tsp. ground cinnamon
1 ½ cups unblanched almonds
3 large eggs
1 tsp vanilla extract
1 tsp almond extract

Preheat oven to 350°.

Cover two cookie sheets with parchment paper.

In a large bowl combine, flour, sugar, baking powder, and cinnamon and stir. Stir in the almonds. Using a whisk, whisk the vanilla into the eggs, and then stir the egg mixture into the flour mixture until you have stiff dough. Turn the dough onto a floured surface and divide into halves. Shape each section into a log, making sure that you shape it fairly smooth. And that it is a little shorter than your baking sheet. Place the rolls onto the baking sheets covered with parchment making sure that they do not touch. Flatten slightly with your hands. Bake about 25 minutes or until logs feel firm when you touch them.

Place the baking pan on a wire rack and let the logs cool completely. When cool, place the logs on a cutting board and cut diagonally in ⅓ inch slices. Place them on the parchment lined cookie sheets and bake them for 10 minutes on one side, turn them over and bake another 10 minutes until lightly golden brown. Let cool completely. These biscotti will stay fresh in an airtight container for several days.

Enjoy
This recipe makes about 60 biscotti.

Made in the USA
Charleston, SC
23 December 2016